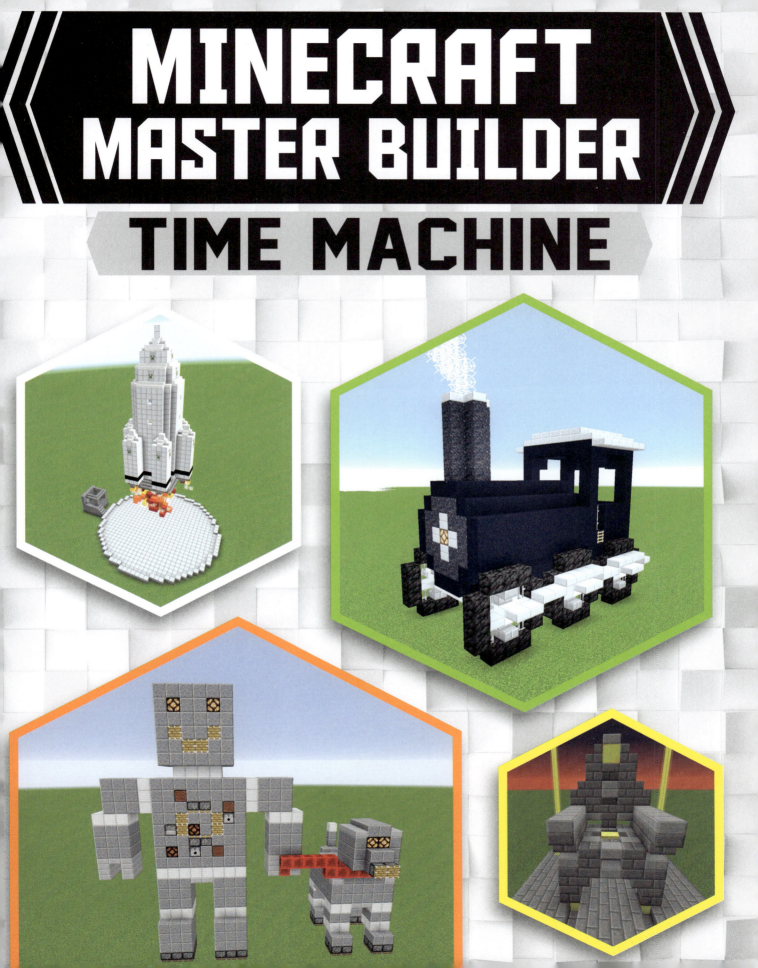

Published in 2020 by Mortimer Children's Books
An imprint of Welbeck Children's Limited,
part of Welbeck Publshing Group.
20 Mortimer Street, London W1T 3JW

Text and design © Welbeck Children's Limited,
part of Welbeck Publishing Group.

This book is not endorsed by Mojang Synergies AB.
Minecraft and Minecraft character names
are trademarks of Mojang Synergies AB.
All screenshots and images of Minecraft
characters/gameplay © Mojang Synergies AB.

All rights reserved. No part of this publication may be
reproduced, stored in a retrieval system, or transmitted
in any form or by any means, electronically, mechanical,
photocopying, recording or otherwise, without
the prior permission of the copyright owners
and the publishers.

A CIP catalogue record for this book is available
from the British Library.

ISBN: 978-1-78312-419-0

Printed in Dongguan, China

7 9 10 8 6

Designed and packaged by:
Dynamo Limited

Builds by:
Jake Turner

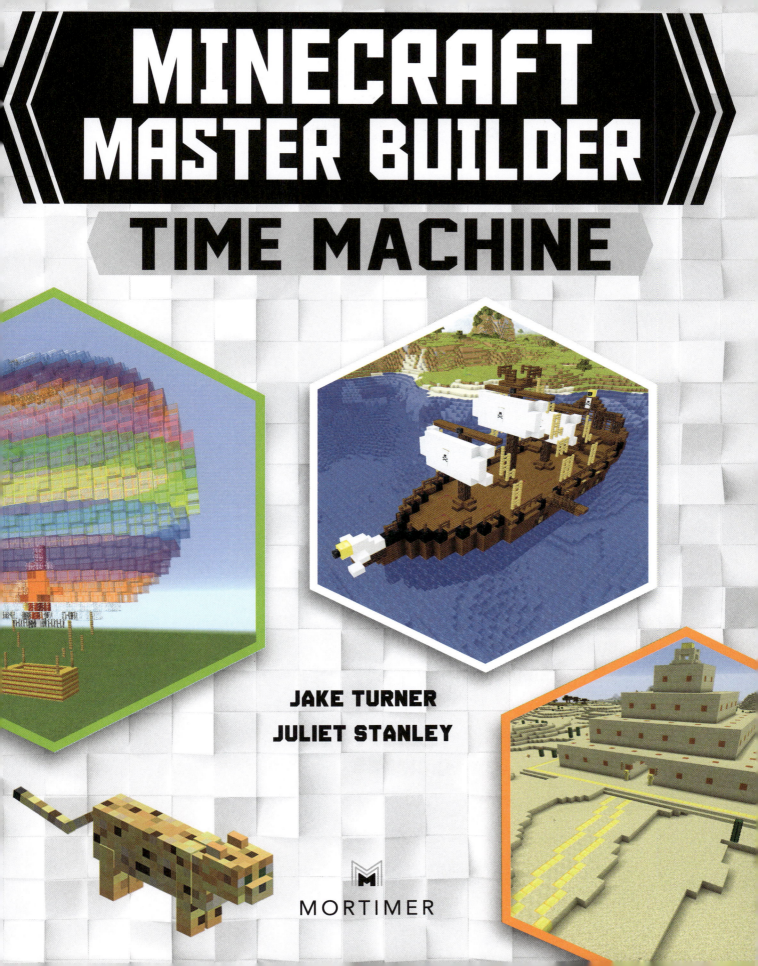

CONTENTS

» Travel Through Time With Minecraft! — 6
» Your Time Machine — 8

PAST POWER — 10
» **Easy build:** Medieval Throne — 12
» **Intermediate build:** Imperial Palace — 14
» **Master build:** Stone Army — 18

AWESOME ARCHITECTURE — 22
» **Easy build:** Pyramid — 24
» **Intermediate build:** Tudor Mansion — 26
» **Master build:** Roman Temple — 30

MARVELLOUS MACHINES — 34
» **Easy build:** Robot — 36
» **Intermediate build:** Booby Trap — 38
» **Master build:** Rocket — 42

TIMELESS TRANSPORT 46

» **Easy build:** Steam Engine 48
» **Intermediate build:** Hot Air Balloon 50
» **Master build:** Pirate Ship 54

FUTURE FANTASTIC 58

» **Easy build:** Eco-house 60
» **Intermediate build:** Hover Bus 62
» **All time master build:** Space Base 66

» **Glossary** 72

TRAVEL THROUGH TIME WITH MINECRAFT!

Ever wondered where you would go if you had a time machine? Well, wonder no more! This book provides a guide to building your own machine and takes you on a time-travelling tour to find fresh ideas for your Minecraft builds.

New to Minecraft? Then it's worth downloading the game and playing it before you read any further. Spend an hour or so meeting mobs and crafting blocks in Survival mode or building in Creative mode, where blocks are pre-made and nasty mobs can't get you. Keep one eye on the clock, though. It's easy to lose track of time when you're having fun (or being chased by zombies)!

ALL SET?
IT'S TIME TO GO!

«WAIT A MINUTE!»

The book is divided into five sections: Past Power, Awesome Architecture, Marvellous Machines, Timeless Transport and Future Fantastic. Each section has three difficulty levels but the very last build has an extra challenge (see below for a clue). With step-by-step instructions, screenshots and expert tips, your Minecrafting skills will sky-rocket in no time.

Courtesy of 'BuildersRefuge'

PYRAMID — 24TH CENTURY BC
12TH CENTURY BC
STONE ARMY — 3RD CENTURY BC
BOOBY TRAP
2ND CENTURY BC
ROMAN TEMPLE — 14TH CENTURY
IMPERIAL PALACE — 15TH CENTURY
MEDIEVAL THRONE — 16TH CENTURY
TUDOR MANSION — 17TH CENTURY
PIRATE SHIP

SUPER SURVIVAL

Mobs are not able to cross rails. Circle the perimeter of your build with powered rails, leaving enough space outside to farm or just enjoy, and you can rest easy in Survival mode. Also, if you place a Minecart on the track, any mobs that approach it will end up on board!

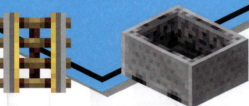

STAYING SAFE ONLINE

Minecraft is one of the most popular games in the world, and we want you to have fun while you're playing it. Just as important as having fun is staying safe when you're online. Here are some top tips for staying safe:

» Keep personal details to yourself
» Only screen share with real-life friends
» Ask a trusted adult before downloading
» Set a game-play time limit
» Tell a trusted adult what you're doing

TEAM-TASTIC

Crafting and building with friends is lots of fun, and when you're in Survival mode it's good to know someone's got your back. Multiplayer can be accessed via the main menu and works by letting players share the same server. Multiplayer doesn't let you pause play but it does allow you to chat. Some of the Minecraft challenges actually require multiple players, so it's a good idea to play this way if your ultimate aim is to win Minecraft.

HOT AIR BALLOON	ROCKET		ECO-HOUSE		SPACE BASE
	19TH CENTURY	21ST CENTURY		22ND CENTURY	
18TH CENTURY	20TH CENTURY		21ST CENTURY		23RD CENTURY
	STEAM ENGINE	ROBOT		HOVER BUS	

7

YOUR TIME MACHINE

DIFFICULTY: INTERMEDIATE

TIME: 2 HOURS

First things first! You can't start your amazing journey across time and space without a time machine, can you? So, the first build of the book is your very own time-travelling mode of transport, so you can surf the centuries in timeless style...

MATERIALS

STEP 1

First, lay the stone slab base for your time machine, with a diameter of 21 blocks. Add iron block around the edge, leaving a gap of seven blocks. In the centre, add four stone slabs to mark the corners of a 7x7 square.

STEP 2

Next, build the control centre in the gap, using stone slab, stone, iron block and blue stained glass pane. Add a stone button and a lever for your control panel.

STEP 3

Build your time-travel pod two blocks above the stone slab markers. Start with a 5x5 blue, orange, lime, yellow and red wool floor. Build two walls three blocks high from red, magenta and blue wool, stone slab and iron door.

STEP 4

Build one of the two walls from wool, grey stained glass pane and quartz stair.

STEP 5

Inside the pod, add a driving seat as well as passenger seating from stone brick stair and a table from stone slab.

STEP 6

In front of the driving seat, build a wool wall with a light blue stained glass pane windscreen in it, plus levers, buttons and tripwire hooks.

STEP 7

Next, complete the roof of the pod with more wool and stone slabs. As you build up each layer of blocks, reduce the size until you are left with one central stone slab at the top.

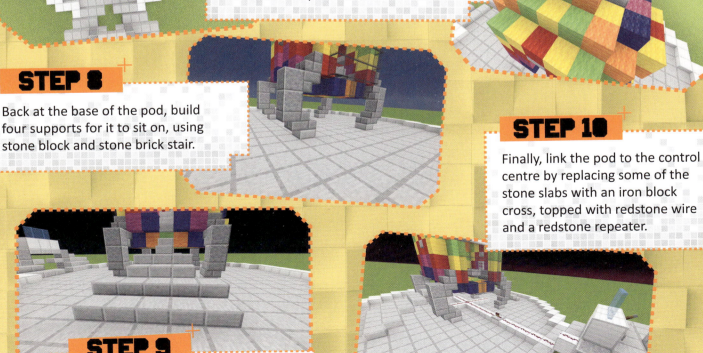

STEP 8

Back at the base of the pod, build four supports for it to sit on, using stone block and stone brick stair.

STEP 9

Leading up to the pod's iron doors, build steps from stone slab.

STEP 10

Finally, link the pod to the control centre by replacing some of the stone slabs with an iron block cross, topped with redstone wire and a redstone repeater.

9

PAST POWER
BIG BUILDINGS, MASSIVE MOBS

Powerful personalities can be very demanding, whether you're an architect working for a tsarina or a Minecrafter fighting mobs. So, let's visit some of the amazing homes that have been created for royalty and meet some of the most powerful mobs from your favourite game. After all, preparation is everything!

« ATTENTION TO DETAIL »

It's the power of Minecraft, not an emperor, that has inspired this regal creation. With its swirling hedgerows and arched windows and doors, you wouldn't think this amazing replica of Versailles, in France, was made from blocks.

« COLD COMFORT »

This stunning build has a central garden like the Winter Palace in St Petersburg, Russia, although it's nowhere near as big! And it's under a glass roof to protect it from the frost. The builder has made the most of the biome – everything is covered in snow!

Courtesy of 'xv12commander'

Courtesy of 'Frelunior'

GRIDLOCK
EXPERT TIP!
Draw a circle on graph paper and then colour in the squares it goes through to work out how to create your Minecraft circles.

⟪ STRONG STYLE ⟫

Lots of tiers and sweeping roofs with ends pointing up at the sky – one look and you know it's a Chinese palace. The builder has copied this iconic style brilliantly. Using a range of different blocks and some well placed iron bars helps to recreate a finish fit for an emperor (or empress!).

Courtesy of 'creepus_killerus'

⟪ MOB MASTERS ⟫

Even in the timeless world of Minecraft, some mobs are more powerful than others. Ender dragons and withers are two of the most powerful and difficult to defeat mobs in Minecraft, but a group of ghasts is also a formidable enemy in Survival mode.

GHAST

These ghastly mobs shoot exploding fireballs and they can spot a player from 100 blocks away! They won't chase you – let's face it, they don't need to – but if there aren't any blocks in the way, they will attack. And they will probably find you before you find them.

WITHER

Withers are Minecraft bosses. Seconds after spawning, they make an explosion which destroys everything close to them. Only after that can you attack them. But beware: they break most blocks they come into contact with and they can't be harmed by fire, lava or water.

ENDER DRAGON

An ender dragon spawns as soon as you arrive in the End and you have to defeat it in order to win the game. Ender dragons were the first Minecraft bosses and although they aren't technically hostile mobs, once roused to battle they are very difficult to defeat.

BLOCK IT OUT

EXPERT TIP!

Use transparent blocks like glass to create a shield from ghasts. Their screams sound the same whether they are near or far so when you hear their high-pitched sounds, start building your shield!

11

PAST POWER
MEDIEVAL THRONE

DIFFICULTY: EASY

TIME: 1 HOUR

With great power comes great responsibility... and probably the need to sit down and have a rest! This throne was inspired by the medieval era, when people believed in the divine right of royalty – they thought that queens and kings were put on the throne by God.

MATERIALS

STEP 1
Create a 10x9 base from stone brick. Add edges, steps and slit details with stone brick stair. Mark where the throne will go with gold block. Place two yellow stained glass blocks at the back.

STEP 2
For the throne legs, place a column of two stone brick blocks on top of the gold blocks. Add two stone brick stairs to the inside of each of these columns to create the seat corners.

STEP 3
Next, build the centre of the seat using a mixture of stone brick stair and stone slab. Place a gold block in the middle – nothing less than gold is good enough for a royal behind!

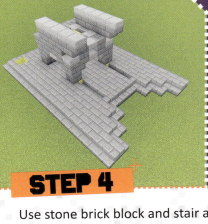

STEP 4

Use stone brick block and stair and stone slab for the arms of your throne. Make sure the arms stick out at the front of the throne, towards the steps.

STEP 5

Build the back of your throne from a combination of stone brick and stone slab, leaving gaps for extra detail and texture.

STEP 6

Decorate the top of the throne with gold block and stone slab.

STEP 7

Dig under the back corners and place 3x3 gold blocks directly underneath both stained glass blocks. Place beacons in the centre of the gold blocks and under the glass to create powerful beams of light. Then replace the grass.

EXPERT TIP!

THINK BIG, BUILD BIGGER!

Like all the best medieval monarchs, this throne is larger than life – about five times bigger in scale than your average Minecraft character. For great detail, it's always best to build BIG!

13

PAST POWER

IMPERIAL PALACE

DIFFICULTY INTERMEDIATE **TIME** 2 HOURS

You aren't afraid of heights, are you? That's good, because this build is pretty high up. Maybe you've noticed that lots of important royal buildings are on hills? That's because they give a good view of any approaching enemies, something that's very useful in Survival mode, too!

MATERIALS

STEP 1

First, terraform to create a level area in your chosen spot. Use cobblestone to build your 36x10 foundation with two rows at the front: 14x1 and 12x1. Stagger the blocks underneath to fit with the mountainside.

STEP 2

Add supports around the sides of your foundation from dark oak wood with dark oak stair at the top and bottom. Space these five blocks apart with two in each corner.

STEP 3

Build the walls from a mixture of quartz and pillar quartz. Make them three blocks high, leaving nine gaps for windows (two blocks high) and one for the door (three blocks high).

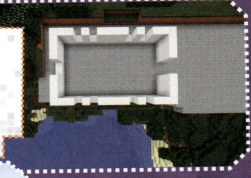

STEP 4

Complete the windows with glass pane and quartz slab windowsills. Top the walls with quartz stair.

STEP 5

Add two horizontal quartz slabs above the door and two more vertical slabs on top of them. Then place quartz stair on either side for decoration.

STEP 6

Make roof supports using two dark oak wood and one dark oak stair. Place two at each corner with a quartz slab in between. Down the long walls, place two supports two blocks apart and five blocks from the corner supports.

STEP 7

Start building the roof on top of your roof supports. Build it six blocks up from the quartz walls. Above the door, add a row of dark oak stair with dark prismarine above it...

...and add gold block underneath the roof for decoration.

15

STEP 8

Complete the roof by adding rows of dark oak wood and dark oak stair.

STEP 9

Build walls in an 11x11 square for the second part of your palace using quartz and pillar quartz. Leave three blocks pushed out at the side, and gaps for six windows and two doors.

STEP 10

Add quartz stair to the top of the walls, glaze the windows and add quartz slab windowsills.

STEP 11

Build a corridor between the two parts of your palace using quartz, quartz pillar, dark oak wood and stair.

STEP 12

Add roof supports and quartz slab corners, as before.

STEP 13

Build your roof three blocks high and complete it with rows of dark oak wood and stair.

STEP 14

On top, build walls three blocks high with six glazed windows and a quartz stair top.

16

STEP 15

Lay a quartz floor level with the wooden roof and...

...then add roof supports to the top of the walls, with quartz slab in each corner.

STEP 16

Add quartz and gold inside the roof supports. Add dark prismarine to the sides of the roof.

STEP 17

Finally complete the top of the roof with dark oak wood, stair and a slab at the top so that it sits five and a half blocks above the quartz walls.

EXPERT TIP!

PRISMARINE

We've used dark prismarine to represent jade – a precious stone in ancient China. In Minecraft, normal prismarine is special because it constantly changes from green to purple to indigo.

PAST POWER
STONE ARMY

DIFFICULTY: MASTER
TIME: 3 HOURS +

Great leaders really do leave lasting impressions. Terracotta armies and pyramids full of riches are just some of the ways they make sure they are never forgotten, even after death.

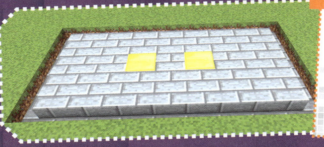

MATERIALS

STEP 1

Dig a 9x5x1 rectangle in the ground. Line the sides with stone brick stair and fill in the rest with stone brick. Then add two gold blocks, one block in from the long sides and two blocks in from the short sides.

STEP 2

Build your soldier from stone, stone brick stair and stone slab with emerald block eyes and a diamond block chest decoration. It should stand nine blocks tall and seven blocks wide. Finally, add a stone brick stair nose!

STEP 3

Lay a 34x20 floor, with staggered edges at one end. Make sure your first soldier stands 11 blocks from the front and three from the side of the floor. Lay an 8x2 path made from gold block covered in red carpet down the centre. Use stone brick stair for the perimeter and the sides of the red carpet. Use stone block at the front of the hall. Then use cobblestone and stone brick for alternate soldiers' platforms.

STEP 4

At the other end of your hall, dig up the ground and lay stone slab, stone brick stair and gold in a symmetrical arrow shape to create an armoury 20 blocks long and 24 blocks wide.

STEP 5

Build stone walls two blocks high around the outside of your hall floor. Add a layer of stone brick stair along the top.

STEP 6

Construct your armoury walls four blocks high from stone brick and cobblestone. Build the entranceway from stone and stone brick stair. Extend cobblestone down the sides of the whole building and join it to the hall with stone slab and stone brick.

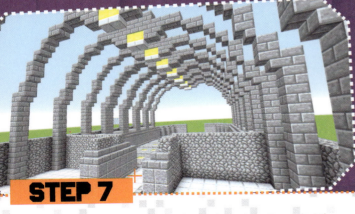

STEP 7

Build the roof arches 16 blocks high, using stone brick and stone brick stair with gold blocks and stone slab for the centrepieces. Make them one block wide in the armoury and two blocks wide in the main hall.

EXPERT TIP!

ROOF RULES

Always start with the roof arches (they go across the build). No matter what shape they are, make sure they are all the same shape. Then simply connect your arches with rows of blocks or stairs.

STEP 8

Make the roof rain-proof by connecting all of the roof arches with rows of cobblestone.

STEP 9

Finish off the back of the armoury with lots of columns of cobblestone, and two columns of stone brick and stone brick stair that reach up to meet the nearest roof arch.

STEP 10

Add a layer of cobblestone to the wall between the armoury and the main hall. Then create a decorative archway that's 10 blocks high, from cobblestone and cobblestone stair.

STEP 11

Back in the main hall, construct your entrance. First, build two stone brick and stone brick stair columns that reach up to meet the nearest roof arch. Then connect them with cobblestone rows. Lastly, create the stone brick and stone brick stair archway.

STEP 12

Follow Step 2 nine times to create nine more soldiers. Make sure the two soldiers at the front have diamond chest decorations and give all the ones behind them gold chest decorations.

STEP 13

Decorate your armoury with item frames, place shelves made from stone brick stair under them and add golden axes and golden swords to them. Next, add golden armour stands and gold block along the walls.

STEP 14

Use a canvas and a painting of a creeper to decorate the entrance to your main hall. Hang these on 2x2 stone square and add a few seats made from stone brick stair.

STEP 15

Build the outside of the entrance to the hall from a combination of stone brick and stone brick stair. Make it 13 blocks high and eight blocks wide.

STEP 16

Finally, extend the path made from stone brick stair and gold block covered with red carpet by 10 blocks so it stretches outside. Section off a 20x11 rectangle using cobblestone wall and build an archway in it that is eight blocks high and seven blocks wide. Then sprinkle bone meal to grow tall grass and flowers.

EXPERT TIP!

KNOCK! KNOCK!

Keep those pesky mobs at bay by adding a fence to the top of the cobblestone wall and also a gate. Moats are always great for stopping mobs in their tracks, too!

AWESOME ARCHITECTURE
STANDING THE TEST OF TIME

From massive, mysterious stone circles to cities that float on water, it seems there's nothing humans won't build. Some of the most stunning structures still exist because we love them so much we won't let them fall down. Others – like the Hanging Gardens of Babylon – exist as legends.

CIRCA 1500

Courtesy of 'Michelle828'

EXPERT TIP!

SKY HIGH
You can build up to 256 blocks high in Minecraft, so make sure you don't plan your builds to go any higher than that.

« OCEAN HOME »

The saying goes that 'Rome wasn't built in a day' but another world-famous Italian city, Venice (above), took more than a millennium to create. People began building houses on top of wooden stilts as far back as the 5th century when Venice was just islands in the sea.

Lucky for you, Minecraft lets you build in mid-air. Seed an ocean biome and set up your own Venice-style city. Your challenge: build it in a day!

What does 'circa' mean?

It comes from the world 'circle' and it means 'round about' or 'roughly'.

Ooh, you're so clever, Alex!

GREEN DREAM

CIRCA 600 BC

Courtesy of 'Gralex'

No one knows exactly where the Hanging Gardens of Babylon were, when they were created or even if they were real... but they are known as one of the Seven Wonders of the Ancient World. Legend has it that these gardens were grown over a towering structure with greenery cascading down off its walls.

There are lots of plants to choose from in Minecraft. Your challenge: build the biggest plant-inspired structure possible.

CIRCA 2000

Courtesy of 'Zeemo'

HEAD IN THE CLOUDS

All it takes is one column of blocks and you can build whatever you like, however big, up in the sky. It's not so easy in the real world, and we are full of admiration for the architects, engineers and builders who created amazing skyscrapers like UOB Plaza, in Singapore.

Your Minecraft challenge: create a tower fit for an ender dragon, spawn one and see what it thinks of your efforts. Top marks to anyone who can get an ender dragon to roost on their rooftop.

SOLID AS A ROCK

No one really knows why there's a huge stone circle in the middle of a grassy plain in England, or how it was built. The stone used for Stonehenge (below) isn't even from the local area – it travelled from many miles away. How the stone got there is another mystery.

CIRCA 2500 BC

Courtesy of 'xxBastet'

Your challenge: create your own mysterious stone structure, and hide the answer to why it is there within its walls, or the ground beneath it. Invite your friends to try and discover its hidden secrets via multiplayer.

BACK STORY

EXPERT TIP!

Come up with a story behind, or at the very least a reason for, your build. Hide treasures and messages within its walls (or in secret rooms underneath it) and get your friends to do the same. It's time to get creative and take charge of multiplayer in Survival!

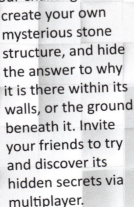

Becoming an architect takes many years of study and training, but Minecraft provides the ultimate short-cut. All you need to do is switch on a device... and turn the page!

AWESOME ARCHITECTURE
PYRAMID

DIFFICULTY EASY **TIME** 1 HOUR

Pyramids are some of the best examples of awesome architecture on Earth. They have stood proud and mysterious in the Egyptian desert for thousands of years. Set the time machine for 2,400 BC and get ready to take notes. It's time to create your own little bit of awesome-ness in just one hour!

MATERIALS

STEP 1
Find a fairly flat desert biome and build a 50x50 foundation in the sand out of gold and sandstone block. Edge your foundation with several rows of sandstone stair until they reach the desert floor.

STEP 2
In one corner, five blocks in from both edges, build a 5x5x5 cube using mostly smooth sandstone with one red chiselled sandstone in the centre of each face. For additional decoration, place chiselled sandstone around each red sandstone block.

STEP 3

Keep repeating Step 2 until you have created the first tier of the pyramid. To create the 4x15 corridor and the 14x15 inner chamber, turn your 5x5x5 cubes into 3x3x5 cuboids.

STEP 4

Repeat Step 2 to build up the next three tiers of your pyramid.

STEP 5

Lay a 6x6 chiselled red sandstone square with a 4x4 smooth sandstone square inside it for your pyramidion to sit on. Place four rows of sandstone stair on top of this, each four blocks long. Add four chiselled sandstone columns, three blocks high, and connect them at the top with sandstone stair. Finally add a 2x2 gold square on top.

STEP 6

Decorate your entrance with golden armour stands and torches on top of oak fence. Make an arched roof from sandstone block and a stair that extends down the corridor.

STEP 7

Furnish your inner chamber with double chests and golden armour stands on gold blocks. Hang item frames containing golden swords above sandstone stair shelves. Add ceiling corner details using gold and sandstone stair. Finally, place a sarcophagus, made from gold and red carpet, on a sandstone stair base that's embedded into the floor.

EXPERT TIP!

SACRED PET

Keep ocelots around your pyramid just like the ancient Egyptians did! You'll need to spawn them as the desert isn't their natural home. Then tame them and feed them fish so that they breed.

25

AWESOME ARCHITECTURE
TUDOR MANSION

DIFFICULTY: INTERMEDIATE

TIME: 2 HOURS

Some building styles are so eye-catching that people carry on copying them for hundreds of years. In Tudor times, houses were a very distinctive black and white colour, and today many houses are still built in the same style. However, plumbing wasn't as good then as it is now, so while the houses might have looked good, the smell inside would have been eye-wateringly bad!

MATERIALS

STEP 1
Replace grass with white concrete to make a T-shape in the ground. Make your T-shape from four 14x14 squares – three in a line with the fourth placed underneath. Place one marker block in each corner of your four squares.

STEP 2
Make each section of the outside walls (except the middle section in the longest side) from white concrete, dark oak wood, dark oak stair and glass pane. Make them five blocks high.

STEP 3

Build a front door in the centre of the middle section in the longest side. Use two dark oak doors with two dark oak slabs above them and with fence and glowstone at the sides.

STEP 4

Use the same materials for your back door – only less of them. Position your back door in the bottom right-hand corner of the T-shape.

STEP 5

Use more white concrete for your internal walls and place doors in the middle of each one. Make these doors three blocks high and two blocks wide.

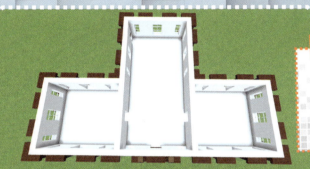

STEP 6

Use the same materials for the inner doors as you used for your front door. Build your staircase using dark oak stair, slab and plank. Make sure you don't block the window and start and finish the staircase three blocks wide.

STEP 7

Leaving a 3x5 gap for your staircase, lay dark oak plank flooring level with the top of your walls. Add a row of white concrete around the edges when you have finished laying the flooring.

STEP 8

Now build the outer walls on the first floor level. These are identical to the ground floor walls, except the middle sets of windows are smaller and the columns on the outside of the windows are two blocks thick.

STEP 9

Build three internal walls with three doors leading out of your upstairs hall. Decorate with paintings, red carpet and a sofa made from oak wood plank and oak wood stair. Add dark oak fence to the sides of your stairway gap and place lighting made from wooden trapdoors and glowstone on top of one end.

STEP 10

In the back room, six blocks in from the door and five blocks in from the side walls, make a 4x7x4.5 bed. Add torches, paintings and oak wood stair seating, side tables and a mirror finished with light blue stained glass pane. Create your own wall art by putting a golden apple in an item frame.

EXPERT TIP!
INSIDE STORY

Decorate the rest of your rooms in the same style as the upstairs hallway and bedroom. Using similar materials and colours throughout your build will make it more stylish.

LIGHT NIGHT

You'll need good lighting around and inside your mansion to make it through the night in Survival mode. Place daylight sensors on top of redstone lamps at regular intervals around your walls.

STEP 11

Add a layer of white concrete on top of the walls to create a ceiling. Build gables in the middle of the front, back and side walls, four blocks high and 12 blocks wide.

STEP 12

Complete your roof using rows of dark oak stair blocks that decrease in size as you build upwards.

29

AWESOME ARCHITECTURE
ROMAN TEMPLE

DIFFICULTY MASTER
TIME 3 HOURS +

MATERIALS

Roman temples contained beautiful art in the form of mosaic floors and statues. Over the centuries, mosaics have been uncovered all over the world. The mosaic in this build is made up of symmetrical shapes and patterns but the Romans created mosaics depicting animals and people, too. What else would you like your mosaic to include?

STEP 1
Create a 40x50 rectangular sandstone base. Build it six blocks high and add steps at the front from descending and extending rows of sandstone and sandstone stair.

STEP 2
Make a column using quartz stair, quartz slab and chiselled quartz. Start with a 3x3 base of quartz stair and slab. Add alternate layers of chiselled quartz and quartz stair. Build it 12 blocks high.

STEP 3

Repeat Step 2 until you have built a total of 32 columns. There should be eight columns along each short side and 10 along the longer sides, with a two block gap between each column.

STEP 4

Build the 30x40 temple walls 12 blocks high to create a 28x38 floor space inside. Use different materials for each layer: sandstone, chiselled sandstone, smooth sandstone or sandstone stair. Leave a 6x4 gap for the entrance.

STEP 5

Create an arched entrance by adding sandstone stair to the top corners of the entrance and removing two more blocks from the top.

STEP 6

Mark the 28x28 square edge of your mosaic floor with cyan stained clay, leaving a 10x28 space at the back of the temple for a plinth for a Roman god.

STEP 7

Build your 10x14 plinth base from quartz and sandstone stair. Add two more rows to create six steps on three sides of the plinth, leading up to a 7x8 quartz and chiselled quartz platform. Add three pillar quartz columns in each corner. Place redstone torches around the walls, eight blocks up and three blocks apart.

EXPERT TIP!

FULL COLOUR SPREAD

Remember there are no less than 16 colours to choose from in certain types of block, such as stained glass, hardened clay (also called terracotta and stained clay), wool, carpet and concrete.

31

STEP 8

Build your Roman god from chiselled quartz, quartz stair, quartz slab and gold. Place it in the centre of the plinth and make it six blocks high.

STEP 9

Inside the 28x28 square, continue your mosaic floor by adding a 20x20 square with a circle inside it. Make your circle using a combination of single and double blocks in a symmetrical pattern.

STEP 10

Lay red, pink, magenta, grey, yellow, lime and light blue stained clay in a symmetrical pattern in the outside edge of your mosaic.

STEP 11

Use cyan, yellow, light blue, lime and pink stained clay to fill in the space between the 20x20 square and the circle with another symmetrical pattern.

STEP 12

Add 12 two-block rows of purple stained clay inside the circle and then four 3x3 squares of lime and light blue hardened clay to leave a sandstone cross shape in the centre.

STEP 13
Complete the last section of the mosaic with pink, red and yellow stained clay.

STEP 14
Build gables at each end of the temple. Starting two blocks in from the walls, add a total of nine rows, each decreasing by one or two blocks each time. Use the same pattern for both ends.

STEP 15
Cover your roof with lots of rows of smooth sandstone in line with the rake of your gable.

STEP 17
Using smooth sandstone, extend the base of your roof so it joins up with the columns around the outside. Extend the blocks in the same pattern over the entrance. Then add another layer of smooth sandstone on top of your roof.

EXPERT TIP!

IRONCLAD
Adding iron doors to the temple entrance will protect you from hostile mobs once you're inside. Don't forget to include a stone button or a lever to provide you with access, though.

33

MARVELLOUS MACHINES
ATTENTION: INVENTION!

Since the beginning of time, humans have been trying to find better ways to survive and thrive. We are constantly inventing new machines to help us understand the world around us, travel faster and further... and have more fun! And Minecraft – itself invented in 2009 – is the perfect place to create and innovate.

Courtesy of 'HappyHaunt'

EXPERT TIP!

RRR! RRR! REDSTONE

You can place redstone wire on blocks by right clicking on the surface of a block while it is selected in your hotbar. Redstone wire cannot be placed on glass. It appears red and sparkling when it is activated.

« FUN TIMES »

All the fun of the fairground really got started at the beginning of the 20th century with electrical power, in the form of carousels, Ferris wheels, dodgem cars and waltzers. In Minecraft, redstone acts like electricity, letting you make circuits and power the movement of different objects. Which fairground ride would you most like to recreate?

MACHINE ON A MISSION

The brick-laying machine, invented in Australia at the beginning of the 21st century, has got to be one of the most useful inventions for busy builders. In Minecraft, only endermen can be relied upon to move blocks, but not in any kind of useful way. Although it is possible to make your own stone factory in Minecraft, the best thing to speed up your build is to find a highly-rated mod.

AIM HIGH

You don't need anything but your imagination to help you build in Minecraft. In the real world, we use lots of different machines to help us construct high buildings. Cranes were first invented in the 6th century BC by the ancient Greeks to help lift heavy materials.

Courtesy of 'Lavaini'

COMPUTER SAYS GO!

You don't need to build big in Minecraft to create a cool machine. The computer below is made with just a few blocks and items. A stylish lamp can be made using a dragon egg for the base and a piston is a Minecraft machine part that is great for making tables. Armed with your imagination and the inventory, the possibilities are endless!

Copyright of 'Crazyhappycool'

Piston   Dragon Egg

GO CLIMB!

EXPERT TIP!

Ladders let you climb any vertical surface. You can make them in Survival mode using seven sticks and your crafting table.

35

MARVELLOUS MACHINES

ROBOT

DIFFICULTY: EASY
TIME: 1 HOUR

Robots are such amazing human creations that one just had to be included here. The first one was made over 2,500 years ago; it was a wooden bird powered by steam. In 1921 the word 'robot' was used for the first time to describe an artificial person. Now robots can walk and talk. This one (well, actually, there are two) doesn't move, but it certainly looks the part.

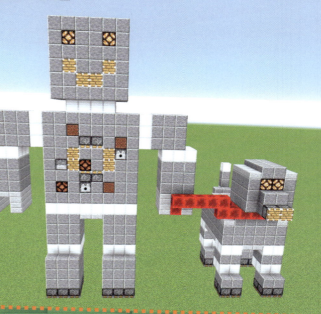

MATERIALS

STEP 1

Feet first! Build two 3x3 squares from upturned pistons, with a gap of two blocks between them. For legs, build two 3x3x3 cubes from polished andesite. One row back, build a 3x3 square from iron block and another polished andesite cube.

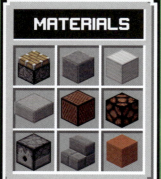
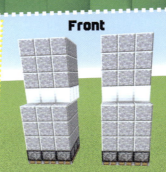

Front · **Back**

STEP 2

Join the top of the legs with 2x3 stone slabs. The robot's body is made from an 8x3 layer of iron block, with an 8x3x8 cuboid of polished andesite on top. Decorate its chest with note blocks, pistons, dispensers and redstone lamps.

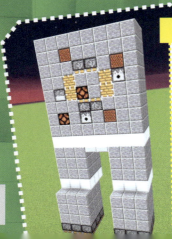

EXPERT TIP!
ROUND THE BLOCK

Positioning blocks so you can present them from a different angle is easier than you might think. Simply try attaching them to the side or underside of other blocks to see if they will show off a different face.

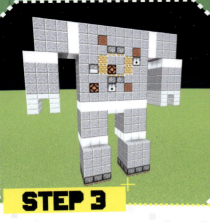

STEP 3

Build your robot's shoulders and arms from 3x3 layers of iron block and 3x3x3 cubes of polished andesite. Make its hands from two 4x3x1 cuboids of stone slab with a 1x3 cuboid in-between.

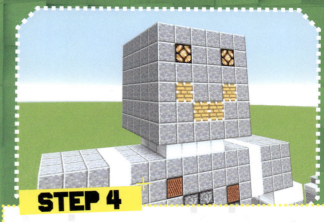

STEP 4

Make your robot's neck from a 4x3 cuboid of iron block. Its head is a 6x6x5 cuboid made from polished andesite. Its eyes are made from redstone lamp and its mouth from pistons.

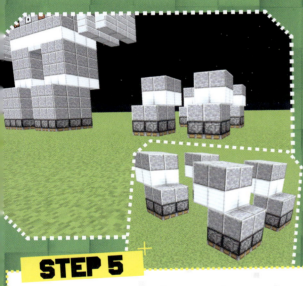

STEP 5

Yes, it's a robot dog! Build its first leg nine blocks away from your robot's foot. Start with four 2x2 squares made from pistons. Space the front legs two blocks apart and the front and back legs four blocks apart.

STEP 6

Make the dog's body from iron block, stone slab and polished andesite. For the tail, use iron block, stone brick stair and polished andesite.

STEP 7

Add a 3x4 redstone collar that sits with one row of blocks sticking out from the front of its body. Place the dog's 4x4x4 head on top, with one row of blocks sticking out at the front. Use redstone lamp for eyes and polished andesite and pistons for the nose. Add another nine redstone blocks to complete the lead.

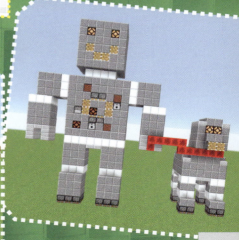

37

MARVELLOUS MACHINES

BOOBY TRAP

DIFFICULTY INTERMEDIATE

TIME 2 HOURS

It may be polite to accept gifts without checking to see if they are any good, but the people of Troy definitely should have checked the horse that was left outside their city gates. It was full of enemy soldiers! What are you going to put inside your horse?

MATERIALS

STEP 1

Make a wheel from oak wood, oak plank and oak stair. Start by placing oak stair on either side of an oak plank and build up from there, leaving an empty block in the centre.

EXPERT TIP!

INSIDE OUT

Fill the interior of this booby trap with armour stands, axes and swords. You might even like to add a few chests filled with supplies for your secret soldiers.

38

STEP 2

Repeat Step 1 until you have four wheels. Leave a gap of 12 blocks between the left-hand and right-hand wheels, and a gap of nine blocks between the edges of the front and back wheels.

STEP 3

Join your front and back wheels with two rows of oak wood that stick out past your wheels by one block. Join these rows together to form the perimeter of a 10x15 base made from oak plank. Cover this in dark oak fence.

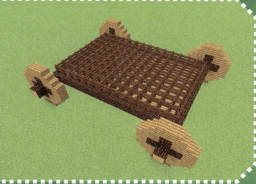

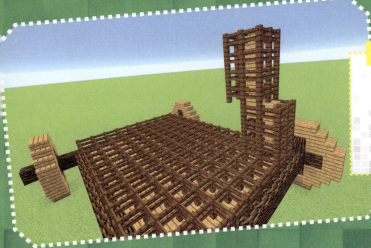

STEP 4

Create one front leg from two columns of oak plank – one three blocks tall and the other four blocks. Place the longer column diagonally behind the shorter one, with a stair block underneath. Surround it with dark oak fence.

STEP 5

Repeat Step 4 so that you have two front legs.

STEP 6

Create one back leg by repeating Step 4. Add a stair block to the top of the bottom column. Then add a column of three blocks to the back of the top column with a stair block underneath.

39

EXPERT TIP!

MAKE A DIFFERENCE

Use several different kinds of wood to give your horse a dappled coat, patches or stripes. You could even turn your booby trap into a unicorn, or give it a saddle and bridle.

STEP 7

Repeat Step 6 so that you have two back legs.

STEP 8

Next, build the hollow 8x17 base for the horse's body using oak plank. Add oak stair underneath to create a rounded shape for its belly.

STEP 9

Add a ladder to the inside of the right-hand back leg with a hole of one block going up into the horse's body.

STEP 10

Complete the body with more oak plank so that it's seven blocks higher than the top of the legs when you've finished. Decorate it with dark oak fence.

STEP 11

Build the horse's neck from oak plank and oak stair with oak wood for decoration. Make it two blocks thick and six blocks high from the top of the horse's body.

STEP 12

Build the horse's head so it's four blocks wide with quartz stair for its eye. Make the head six blocks long and eight blocks tall, including the ears, using a combination of oak stair and plank.

STEP 13

Use gold block and quartz stair to create your horse's mane and tail. Make both two blocks wide.

MARVELLOUS MACHINES
ROCKET

DIFFICULTY MASTER

TIME 3 HOURS+

What can be more marvellous than a machine that can quite literally take you out of this world? (We gave the answer away in the title, didn't we?) The race to develop rockets got off the ground in the 1960s and the two countries that led the race were the U.S.A. and Russia.

MATERIALS

STEP 1
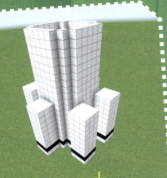
Twenty blocks above the ground, build the footprint for the central cylinder of your rocket and the six boosters that go around it. Use iron blocks for this.

STEP 2
Using iron blocks, build the walls of your central cylinder 20 blocks high. Then build the walls of your boosters 10 blocks high. Use black concrete powder for the second layer from the bottom.

STEP 3

Taper the tops of your boosters using four quartz stair blocks around a central iron block with another iron block on top.

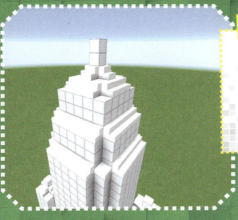

STEP 4

Add the tapered top to your central cylinder, using a combination of quartz stair, quartz slabs and iron blocks. Make it 10 blocks tall in total.

EXPERT TIP!

CRAFTY!

What can you make with a white banner, lime dye and a creeper head? Place them all on a crafting table to make an awesome, if slightly scary, flag!

STEP 5

Decorate the outside of your rocket with banners and add some windows by replacing the iron blocks with glass panes.

STEP 6

Inside your rocket, build three floors using glowstone. Add the first floor five blocks down from where the top of your rocket starts to taper off, the next floor four blocks down from that and the last floor another six blocks down.

STEP 7

The top room is the command module. Equip it with levers and stone buttons, viewing screens made from blue stained glass panes, seats from quartz stair and desks from quartz stair and slabs.

STEP 8

The next module down is the living area. Furnish it with beds placed over iron blocks, side tables made from quartz stair and armour stands for the astronauts' suits.

SWEET DREAMS

Even in Minecraft, finding the right place to settle down for a snooze is important. Beds cannot go on glowstone, snow, ice, glass, carpet or non-solid blocks such as leaves.

STEP 9

Add ladder in one corner of the living area and remove one glowstone block from the floor and ceiling to provide the astronauts with access to all areas. Then add bookshelves and furnaces to complete the living area.

STEP 10

The next level down is the lunar module, which contains a moon buggy. Make your 6x4 moon buggy from iron blocks, black concrete powder, stone slabs and quartz stair with two iron doors at the front.

STEP 11

Inside your moon buggy, add a lever and a stone button to open your iron doors, with a blue stained glass viewing screen and a desk and chair made from quartz stair with a stone slab table behind them.

STEP 12

For your engine, first build a column of iron blocks from floor to ceiling in the centre of the last module. Use redstone for the top block. Add four pistons around the column. Place lapis lazuli on top. Then add more pistons on top of that.

STEP 13

Place four stone brick stairs under each booster to create the booster motors.

STEP 14

Use more stone slabs for the central rocket motor. Start with a 4x4 layer and create five more layers to end with a 9x9 layer at the bottom. Complete the underside with quartz slabs.

STEP 15

Create the sensation of a dramatic take-off by adding red, yellow and orange wool blocks surrounded by cobwebs coming out from the bottom of your rocket. We have lift off!

STEP 16

Build a circular launch pad below your rocket, with double stone slabs around the edge and stone slabs in the centre. Give it a diameter of 31 blocks.

STEP 17

Next to your launch pad, build a control centre from stone brick stair, stone brick and stone brick slabs. Use grey stained glass block for the windows and the roof, blue stained glass pane inside for viewing screens and finish with an iron door.

TIMELESS TRANSPORT

ZOOM! ZOOM! ZOOM!

Minecraft travel relies on horses, Minecarts and... pigs! Horses need to be tamed and Minecarts need a rail system. All you need to enjoy a piggyback ride is a rod, a carrot and a saddle. But we reckon you'd like to have a go at creating some of your own transport.

« PERFECTLY PLANE »

The first plane took flight in 1903 and over the last century planes have become a part of our everyday lives, whether they're flying overhead or taking us on holiday. Creating your own plane in Creative mode is easy. Just build a column of blocks to the height you want and then begin.

Courtesy of 'AlejandrooCraxD29'

EXPERT TIP!

AIRCRAFT MOD-EL

You'll need a mod to create a plane that can fly. Always check out the reviews and make sure you have an adult's permission to download a new mod.

« OLD-FASHIONED FUN »

Cars were invented at the end of the 19th century. The first ones only travelled at around 10 mph (16 km/h) but nowadays the fastest racing cars can reach over twenty times that speed! You can build a moving car on Minecraft with redstone and sticky pistons – it won't go fast (or smoothly!) and it might look a bit vintage, but it'll be yours!

Courtesy of 'Beanteddo'

EXPERT TIP!

PONY PERSONALITY

Each Minecraft horse has a different character – some are easy to tame and others are stubborn. All of them will let you put a lead on them, but climbing onto their back is another matter. A golden apple will always help you make friends.

ROTOR MOTOR

Helicopters started taking to the skies at the beginning of the 20th century, although the Italian artist and inventor Leonardo da Vinci drew designs for a simple helicopter back in the 15th century. Helicopters are great in tight spaces because they can take off and land vertically, as well as hover in the air. They are often used for search and rescue at sea and in the mountains. Can you build one to patrol the Minecraft skies?

Courtesy of 'RaakHeavy'

Inside

Courtesy of 'GetTrapped'

DEEP DOWN

A Dutch engineer, Cornelius Drebbel, built the first usable submarine in 1620. Submarines are often used by the military for secret missions. Scientists also use them to explore the ocean underworld. If you would like to create your own submarine deep below the surface, you'll have to be prepared to remove a lot of water blocks. Sponges at the ready!

TIMELESS TRANSPORT

STEAM ENGINE

DIFFICULTY: EASY **TIME: 1 HOUR**

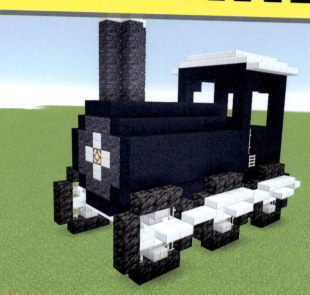

Whether they're trainspotters or not, people often stop to wave when a steam train comes chugging past. These impressive steam-powered machines were invented in Britain in the early 19th century. You can create a magnificent steam locomotive yourself in Minecraft.

MATERIALS

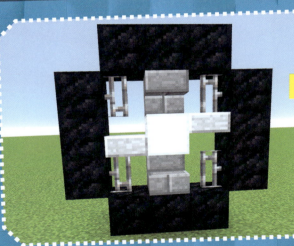

STEP 1

First, build one 5x5 wheel from coal block, stone brick stair, stone slab and iron bars with one iron block in the centre.

STEP 2

Build the rest of your wheels in exactly the same way. Leave a gap of seven blocks between the two rows of wheels and a gap of one block between each adjacent wheel.

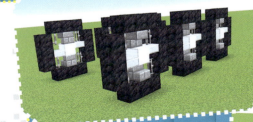
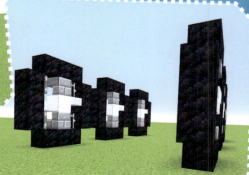

STEP 3

Create a chassis. Connect the centre of each wheel with the wheel opposite using rows of iron block seven blocks long. Join these rows with a central column of iron blocks. On top of your chassis add a 15x5 flatbed made from black concrete.

STEP 4

For the engine, first build a 3x1 row of black concrete onto one end of the flatbed. Add a 3x1 row of black concrete powder and a cross made from double stone slab and redstone lamp above this. Surround the cross with black concrete powder and add black concrete to each long side and in each corner. Extend this shape back 12 blocks so it stops at the back of the second set of wheels.

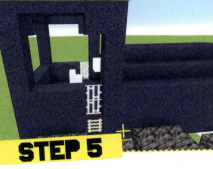

STEP 5

Make the driver's cabin ten blocks high with ladder steps up to it, iron bars side doors, a stone brick stair seat and an iron block steering wheel. Build the roof from stone slab.

STEP 6

For the steam funnel at the front of the engine, make a cross from black concrete powder and build it five blocks high. Top this with stone slab and finish off with steam made from cobwebs.

EXPERT TIP!

POWDER FALL

Concrete powder is affected by gravity. So, if you place it on a non-solid block, like air, it will fall through. In Survival, this means that players and mobs can be suffocated by it. Treat it with care!

STEP 7

Finally, add connecting rods along the sides of the wheels made from stone slabs.

TIMELESS TRANSPORT

HOT AIR BALLOON

DIFFICULTY: INTERMEDIATE **TIME: 2 HOURS**

Hot air balloon trips are as popular as ever, but the first passenger-carrying flight in a hot-air balloon took place in France in 1783. That's a pretty long time ago! Isn't it time a new balloon took to the skies? Here's a rainbow-inspired one for you to try...

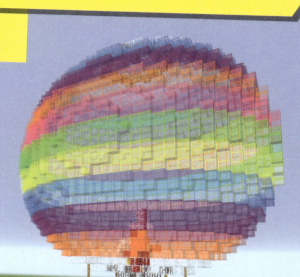

MATERIALS

STEP 1

Build the basket ten blocks above the ground. Use hay bale and make it 7x7x3. Leave a 2x1 gap for the entrance and add ladder below it and oak fence to make it safe.

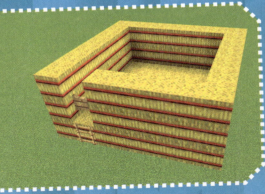

STEP 2

Six blocks above the basket, build a 9x9 diamond shape from glass blocks.

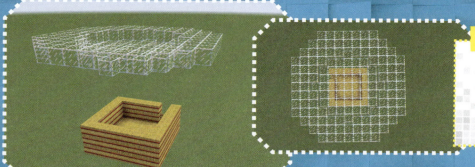

STEP 3

Add another wider layer on the outside edge of your diamond shape. Make it two or three blocks wider all the way around.

STEP 4

Now, add another even wider layer on the outside edge of your last layer. As before, make it two or three blocks wider all the way around.

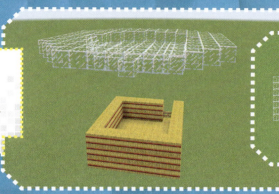

STEP 5

Add three widening layers of orange stained glass block. Make the first from rows that are nine, three and two blocks long. Make the second from rows that are five, four and two blocks long. Make the third from rows that are five, three and two blocks long.

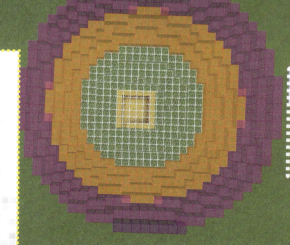

STEP 6

Next, add the magenta layers. Make the first from rows that are three, four and two blocks long with some single blocks. Make the second from rows that are nine and two blocks long with some single blocks. Make the third from rows that are seven, three and two blocks long with some single blocks.

STEP 7

Add the light blue layers. Make the first from rows that are 11 and two blocks long with some single blocks. Make the second from rows that are three and two blocks long with some single blocks. Make the third from rows that are nine, three and two blocks long with some single blocks.

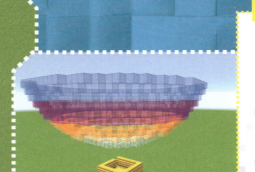

STEP 8

Add the yellow layers. Make the first from rows that are five and two blocks long with some single blocks. Make the second from rows that are five, four and two blocks long with some single blocks. Make the third from rows that are seven, three and two blocks long with some single blocks.

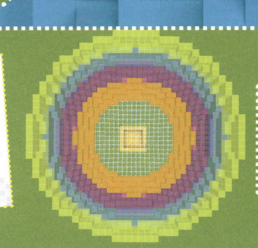
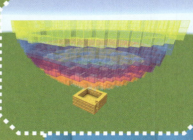

STEP 9

Add one layer of lime stained glass block that is three blocks high. Make it from rows that are seven, three and two blocks long with some single blocks.

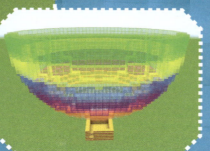

EXPERT TIP!

COUNT ON IT

Iron blocks are really useful when you need to work out the spaces between things – especially if you're building above the ground. They have dark edges so you can count each one easily.

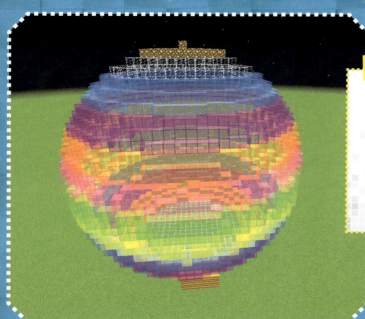

STEP 10

Repeat Step 8 with pink stained glass, Step 7 with more orange stained glass, Step 6 with more magenta, Step 5 with light blue stained glass, Step 4 and 3 with glass block and Step 2 with glowstone. Then add a single block to the very top of the balloon.

STEP 11

Remove the 9x9 circle at the base of the balloon. Add iron bars to four equidistant points and link them to a central iron block. Then add ropes made from fence connecting the balloon basket to the balloon.

STEP 12

Add some fire above the iron block inside the balloon, using red and orange wool and cobweb.

EXPERT TIP!

SUPERCOOL LIQUID

Some people argue that glass isn't a solid at all, but a supercool liquid. (Old window panes are thicker at the bottom than at the top!) The makers of Minecraft agree – blocks that need solid surfaces, like beds, ladders and rails, cannot be placed on glass.

TIMELESS TRANSPORT

PIRATE SHIP

DIFFICULTY: MASTER

TIME: 3 HOURS+

What an adventurous way to spend your days, travelling the seas in search of hidden treasure! And, urm, fighting and stealing? Being a pirate wasn't really a dream job but there were still plenty of them between the late 17th and early 18th century. They had fine and fast ships designed for chasing after boats and then racing away with their victims!

MATERIALS

STEP 1

First, build the base for your pirate ship from dark oak wood planks. Make a 13x22 rectangle and add a prow at the front. Your footprint should sit two blocks high off the waterline.

STEP 2

Extend your footprint three blocks below the waterline and then remove the water from the inside of the boat.

EXPERT TIP!

SOAK IT UP

The best way to remove water from an underwater build is to use sponge, or fill the space with sand or dirt so it soaks up the water and then you can dig it out easily with a shovel.

STEP 3

One block in and down from the bottom of the ship, add a row of blocks from the prow to the stern of the ship. Then one block in and down, add another row. Finally, one more block in and down, build the bottom of your boat.

STEP 4

Section off six 4x4 sleeping areas at the back of the ship. Furnish them with tables made from oak wood stair, beds and an oak door.

STEP 5

Fill your galley with furniture made from oak wood plank and stair. Build a ladder in one corner. Add furnaces (with levers so you can turn them on), a dispenser, a note block, a cauldron and an oak door into your storage area. Fill this with double chests, melon, gold and diamond blocks, carved pumpkin, skeleton skulls and redstone wire for blood!

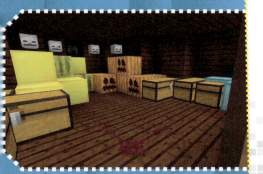

STEP 6

Next, add five portholes down each side of the ship. Make them from dark oak wood and glass pane.

STEP 7

Build your deck on the same level as the top of the portholes, using dark oak plank. Then build up the stern of the ship by adding rows of dark oak plank and upside-down dark oak stair all along the back of the ship.

STEP 8

Next, add rows of upside-down dark oak stair along the sides of the ship. Make these three blocks long, with one coal block between them and extra at the ship's prow. Leave a gap on the port (left) side. Top them with dark oak fence.

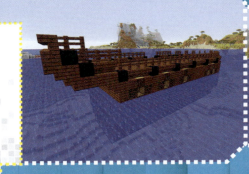

STEP 9

Build three masts from dark oak wood, dark oak wood stair and dark oak wood slab. Make the main mast 12 blocks high and the other two nine blocks high. Add yards made from dark oak wood slab five blocks down from the top of each mast.

STEP 10

Next, add a 9x4 main sail made from white wool.

STEP 11

Make the sails for the other masts in exactly the same way using the same dimensions.

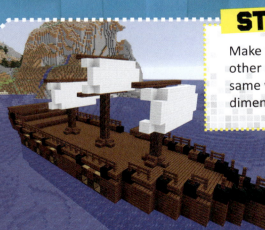

STEP 12

Add a figurehead to the prow of your pirate's ship, made from quartz block, quartz slab and gold.

STEP 13

Build a raised platform level with the top of the stern using dark oak plank and dark oak stair.

STEP 14

Next, add a helm so that the captain can steer the ship. Use dark oak slab, dark oak wood and gold block for this.

STEP 15

Decorate the stern with dark oak wood, fence and stair with a gold block on the top. Pirates like to show off a bit!

STEP 16

Create a crow's nest at the top of the main mast. First, add ladder all the way up. Then make a viewing platform from dark oak stair, slab and fence.

STEP 17

Add rigging all over the boat, made from fence. Pirates need to be able to climb all over the boat when they are fighting and spying!

STEP 18

No pirate ship would be complete without a plank to walk. Make this one using dark oak wood, fence and stair.

STEP 19

Finally, complete the swashbuckling look by adding a skull and cross bones to your sails. Make them by placing a white banner, a wither skeleton skull and an ink sac on a crafting table. Place wither skeleton skulls on the gold blocks on the stern and the prow, and add blood (redstone wire) to your deck.

FUTURE FANTASTIC
WHAT NEXT?

No one is sure what the future holds. We may be driving hover cars in the next few years. Robots could be doing our jobs. We might all be living on another planet. Until we know for sure, there's somewhere we can let our dreams for the future run wild... Minecraft!

EXPERT TIP!
BEST BIOME
The forest biomes are a great place to start playing in Survival mode because wood is easy to mine, so you can build a shelter quickly.

UP, UP AND AWAY!

Have you ever looked up at the night sky and seen the International Space Station flash by? Well, the first ever human-made object to start orbiting Earth was the Russian Sputnik in 1957. Since then more than 8,000 more Earth objects – from satellites and telescopes to much smaller things like nuts and bolts forgotten by astronauts – have gone into orbit.

Your challenge: Design the next object to orbit Earth.

Courtesy of 'Mortill'

Courtesy of 'lava–style'

ON ANOTHER PLANET

Earth is the only planet we can survive on at present but one day we could be living on another planet, such as Mars. Meeting up with family might be a problem though – Mars is over 55 million kilometres away! It's also very cold and we can't breathe in its atmosphere.

Your challenge: Build a house fit for life on Mars. Blocks of lava might be a good idea for keeping warm!

Courtesy of 'Erick97'

« LIVING THE DREAM »

What's your dream house? Does it have a pool? Where is it? How many rooms does it have? These are probably questions you asked yourself when you saw your first biome. In the real world, houses of the future will use renewable resources and be designed to save energy. Looking after the planet is a big priority!

Your challenge: Build your future home, complete with a garage for your environmentally-friendly hover car.

WATER TIGHT

If you're thinking of creating any rooftop water features, whether they're pools, fountains or ponds, make sure that there are at least two layers of solid blocks underneath them. This will stop any drips and leaks.

EXPERT TIP!

« THE ROAD AHEAD »

We may not be using petrol-powered cars in the future but we will still need transport to get around. How will we tackle the problem of busier and busier roads? What will the roads of the future look like?

Your challenge: Create a superhighway junction of the future with at least ten lanes.

Courtesy of 'TheLakitu'

FUTURE FANTASTIC
ECO-HOUSE

DIFFICULTY EASY | **TIME** 1 HOUR

Looking after the environment gets more and more important every day, as the number of people on the planet grows and its natural resources get used up. Nowadays, scientists and designers are constantly coming up with ground-breaking ideas for saving resources and treating the planet with more kindness. And there's nothing better than Minecraft for being green when you're building!

MATERIALS

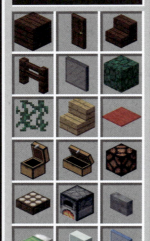

STEP 1

Start by building a 15x15 square floor made from dark oak plank. There's no need to dig up the grass, just place your floor on top!

STEP 2

Build the walls another six blocks high. Add a dark oak front door with a dark oak stair leading up to it and dark oak fence on either side. Add 3x1 windows; five at the front and six at the back and glaze them with grey stained glass pane.

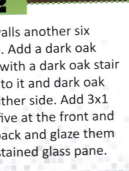

STEP 3

Add jungle leaves and vines in a random pattern around all the walls of your house.

STEP 4

Add a ceiling three blocks up from the floor. Furnish your open-plan downstairs area using oak stair, red carpet, chests and redstone lamp with daylight sensors on top, plus furnaces with a stone button to power them.

STEP 5

Add stairs on one inside wall of the house and make a 4x1 opening in the ceiling to accommodate them. On the second floor, place dark oak fence along two sides of the opening as a safety barrier.

STEP 6

Upstairs, add your ceiling. Then create a bedroom area with two lime beds, oak wood stair side tables and more lighting using redstone lamp and daylight sensors. Use quartz stair and light blue stained glass pane to create your bathroom. Add flowers in pots and an oak wood seating area, too.

 **EXPERT TIP!**

GROW YOUR OWN

Create a kitchen garden full of tasty crops and carrots at the front of your house! This one is surrounded by fence and has cauldrons filled with water and lighting to help the seeds grow.

STEP 7

Cover your roof with grass block and sprinkle this with bone meal to get longer grass and flowers. Add an irregular shape using more grass block and fill it with water to create a wildlife sanctuary.

61

FUTURE FANTASTIC
HOVER BUS

DIFFICULTY INTERMEDIATE **TIME** 2 HOURS

Can you remember being stuck in traffic during the school run? Well, here's a super cool solution – the hover bus! This vehicle can rise above the jam and take you to your destination in no time at all. Hover cars have already been invented but they are not on the road yet so it could be a while before you see one. Still, here's what a hover bus of the future may look like...

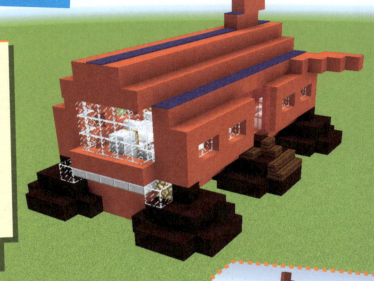

MATERIALS

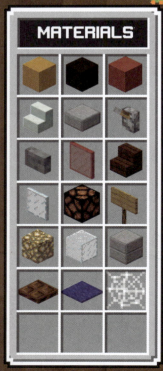

STEP 1

Build six booster jets 10 blocks off the ground, leaving a gap of three blocks between each one. Make a 3x3 square of yellow stained clay. Add a row of black stained clay along each side. On top, add a 3x3 square of black stained clay and a single block.

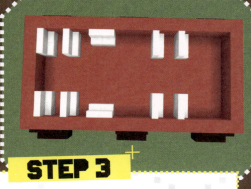

STEP 2

Next, join the bottom of each booster with short rows of red stained clay. Connect the top of each booster with more rows. Join these top and bottom rows to create the two flat ends of the bus and its staggered sides. Add the floor of the bus one block down from the top.

STEP 3

Create seating using quartz stair.

STEP 4

Make the base for the driver's seat using stone slab, three blocks wide and two blocks deep. Use red stained clay and quartz stair for the seat itself and make a 3x1 dashboard from stone slab with a lever and a stone button for controls.

STEP 5

Directly above the middle boosters on either side of your bus, remove the middle three blocks from the top row of red stained clay. Then build doors that are three blocks high from red stained glass pane and steps up to them from dark oak stair.

STEP 6

Add four windows made from glass pane down each side of the bus. Make each window two blocks wide. Add red stained clay between them and in a row above them.

STEP 7

Create the back of the bus using more glass pane and red stained clay. Make it six blocks high. Add lights made from redstone lamp and a sign so you can show where the bus is going.

sign

STEP 8

At the front of the bus, add an extra row of red stained clay five blocks long, with stone slab underneath. Build the windscreen on top three blocks high, with another row of red stained clay on top. Complete the rest of the front of the bus so it is the same shape as the back of the bus. Add headlights made from glowstone behind glass block.

STEP 9

Back inside the bus, remove the row of red stained clay directly in front of the dashboard. Add two double stone slabs in front of the driver's seat with a wooden trapdoor for a steering wheel.

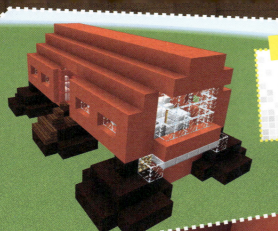

STEP 10

Create a roof for the bus by joining its two curved ends with rows of red stained clay.

STEP 11

Add three stripes along the roof made from blue carpet.

STEP 12

Add fins to the top and sides of the back of the bus. Make the top fin four blocks high. Make each side fin four blocks wide and four blocks deep.

EXPERT TIP!

CLEVER COBWEB

Add cobwebs under each booster to give an impression of their powerful upward thrust. Cobwebs are also good at pretending to be smoke from a chimney and you can even use them as net curtains in a cottage window.

FUTURE FANTASTIC
SPACE BASE

DIFFICULTY: ALL TIME MASTER **TIME: 3 HOURS+**

Planet Earth is getting pretty overcrowded. But can you imagine living in space? At the moment astronauts on the International Space Station can't just pop out for a game of football as they'd float away, and let's not think about how they go to the toilet! In the future these sorts of problems may be fixed and we could be living up near the stars...

MATERIALS

STEP 1
First, build a circular base that's two blocks thick with a diameter of 51 blocks made from iron blocks. Place a glowstone block in the centre surrounded by circle made from sea lantern with a diameter of 13 blocks.

STEP 2
Create the first 9x8x10 living pod using iron block, sea lantern and blue stained glass pane. Add steps made from quartz stair and an iron door in the left-hand corner of the building.

66

STEP 3

Add a layer of iron block to the ground floor of the pod. Then add floors directly above each row of windows to create three floors. Create stairs between each floor using quartz stair. Furnish the ground floor sitting room with an oak wood stair sofa, a blue stained glass pane TV and red carpet.

View of sitting room from front door

STEP 4

Furnish the second floor kitchen with oak wood stair, quartz stair, a dispenser and some furnaces. Furnish the top floor bedroom with red beds, quartz stair, a blue stained glass pane mirror and a lever for a light switch.

View of kitchen from top of stairs

View of top floor bedroom from top of stairs

STEP 5

Repeat steps 2, 3 and 4 three more times, so you have four living pods on your space base.

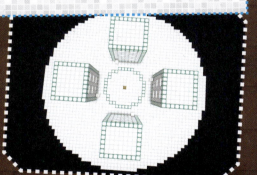

STEP 6

Replace the blocks around the circumference of the space base with sea lantern, grass block and more sea lantern. Then add paths made from eight diagonal rows of sea lantern.

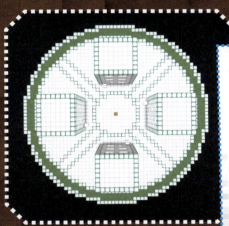

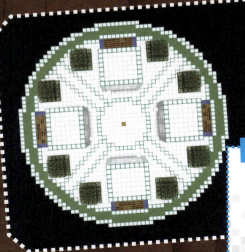

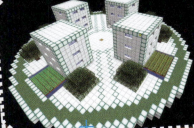

STEP 7

Place trees on either side of each living pod and create crop beds behind them, using 5x7 dirt blocks with rows of water on either side. Add seeds to grow your wheat and potato crops.

EXPERT TIP!

WATER AND LIGHT

To make sure your crops thrive, add extra light and make sure you keep adding water, just like in the real world!

67

STEP 8

Add glass block around the outside of the circumference of the space base.

STEP 9

Build up your glass block wall until it is five blocks high all the way around.

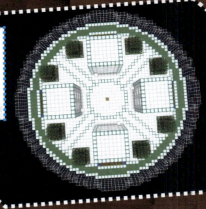

STEP 10

Add extra vertical layers to the long sides of the wall to create a more rounded shape.

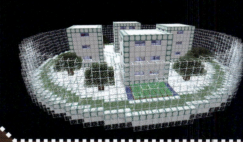

STEP 11

Complete your symmetrical glass dome by reducing the size of the wall by one or two blocks at every layer.

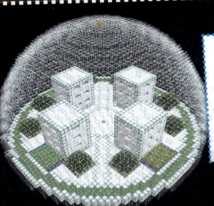

STEP 12

Eight blocks down, follow Step 1 to create another circular base the same size as the first one from iron block.

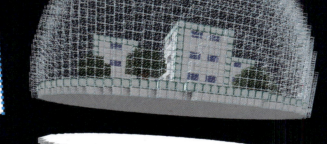

STEP 13

Remove a 5x5 square from the centre of the upper level of the space base and add a spiral staircase up from the lower level, using quartz slab around a glowstone central column.

68

STEP 14

Replace the circle of iron block around the top of the staircase with sea lantern.

STEP 15

Extend the circle of sea lantern down around the spiral staircase. At the bottom, leave a gap that's two blocks high so you can get to the lower level.

STEP 16

Add oak fence around the top of the spiral staircase as a safety barrier.

STEP 17

Next, join the two levels of your space base with 12 columns. Place columns made from iron block, stone brick stair and glowstone at the ends of each straight edge. Place columns made from iron block, stone slab and glowstone in the middle of each curved edge.

STEP 18

Starting at the end of each straight edge, replace the iron block with sea lantern to create four right angles on the floor of your lower level.

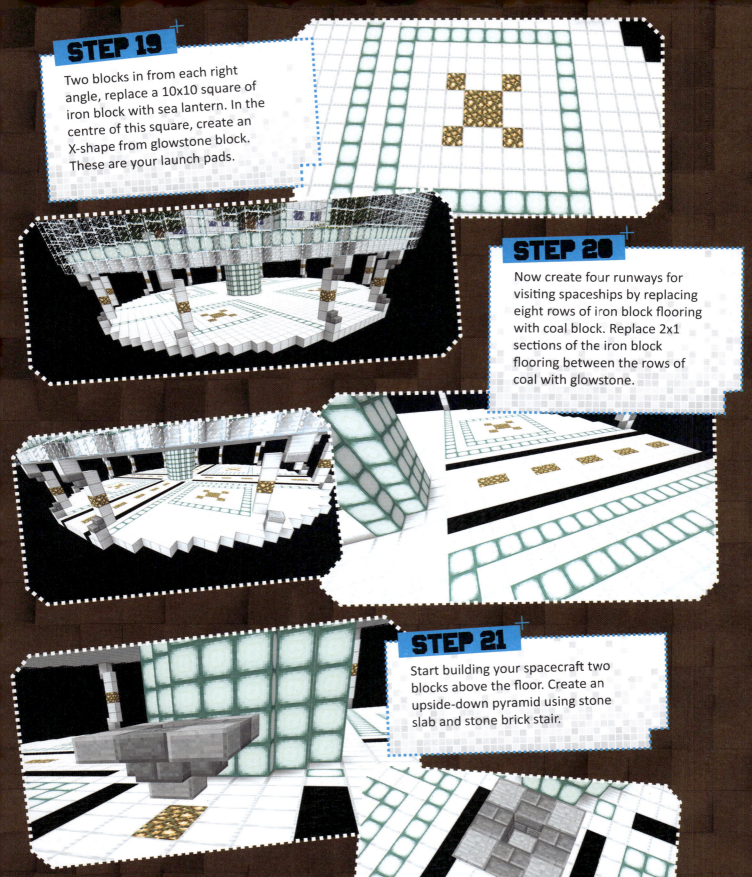

STEP 19

Two blocks in from each right angle, replace a 10x10 square of iron block with sea lantern. In the centre of this square, create an X-shape from glowstone block. These are your launch pads.

STEP 20

Now create four runways for visiting spaceships by replacing eight rows of iron block flooring with coal block. Replace 2x1 sections of the iron block flooring between the rows of coal with glowstone.

STEP 21

Start building your spacecraft two blocks above the floor. Create an upside-down pyramid using stone slab and stone brick stair.

STEP 22

Add a booster to each corner of your spacecraft made from a piston block topped with a stone slab.

STEP 23

Add glowstone lights, a blue stained glass control panel and a creeper driver to your spacecraft. Then use glass block to build a pyramid shape to complete the top. Make sure there is no glass block above your boosters.

STEP 24

Repeat Steps 21–23 to create more spacecraft.

GLOSSARY

《 **BIOME** 》
A region in Minecraft world with special geographical features, plants and weather conditions.

《 **BOSS** 》
A powerful enemy you have to fight in a computer game. Defeating them often means you reach a higher level in the game.

《 **CHASSIS** 》
The frame at the base of a car or other vehicle.

《 **CIRCUMFERENCE** 》
The distance around the edge of a circle.

《 **DIAMETER** 》
The distance from one side of a circle, passing through its mid point, to the other.

《 **EQUIDISTANT** 》
An equal distance apart.

《 **FLATBED** 》
The long, flat structure that lies just above the chassis of a train or truck.

《 **GABLE** 》
The top of the triangular shape at either end of a roof.

《 **GALLEY** 》
The name for a ship's kitchen.

《 **MOB** 》
Short for 'mobile', a mob is a moving creature within the game. Some are tameable, such as wolves, and some are hostile, such as creepers.

《 **MOSAIC** 》
A design or picture made from small pieces of coloured tile, stone or glass.

《 **ORBIT** 》
The repeated movement of an object around a planet.

《 **PLINTH** 》
A raised platform for a special object or statue.

《 **PROW** 》
The front of a ship.

《 **PYRAMIDION** 》
The very tip of a pyramid.

《 **RENEWABLE RESOURCES** 》
Resources (such as wood, wind energy or solar power) that do not run out over the course of time.

《 **SARCOPHAGUS** 》
A coffin made from stone.

《 **STERN** 》
The back of a ship.

《 **TERRAFORM** 》
To prepare the ground before you start building, by digging it up or adding extra blocks.

《 **TSAR** 》
A male Russian ruler before 1917.

《 **TSARINA** 》
A female Russian ruler (or the wife of a Russian ruler) before 1917.

《 **YARD** 》
A horizontal length of wood that sticks out from a ship's mast.